WAR PLANES

Jump Jets:
The AV-8B Harriers
by Bill Sweetman

DISCARD

CAPSTONE
HIGH-INTEREST
BOOKS

an imprint of Capstone Press
Mankato, Minnesota

Capstone High-Interest Books are published by Capstone Press
151 Good Counsel Drive, P.O. Box 669, Mankato, Minnesota 56002
http://www.capstone-press.com

Library of Congress Cataloging-in-Publication Data
Sweetman, Bill.
    Jump jets: the AV-8B Harriers/by Bill Sweetman.
    p. cm.—(War planes)
    Includes bibliographical references and index.
    Summary: Discusses the AV-8B Harrier, its uses, engine, weapons, and
future in the U.S. Marine Corps.
    ISBN 0-7368-1068-4
    1. Harrier (Jet fighter plane)—Juvenile literature. 2. United States. Marine
Corps—Aviation—Juvenile literature. [1. Harrier (Jet fighter plane)] I. Title.
II. Series.
UG1242.F5 S949 2002
623.7'464—dc21   2001003061

Editorial Credits
Carrie Braulick, editor; Timothy Halldin, cover and interior designer; Katy
    Kudela, photo researcher

Photo Credits
Boeing Management Company, 28
Edwards AFB History Office, 7, 26
Photri-Microstock, 9, 18
Ted Carlson/Fotodynamics, cover, 1, 4, 10, 13, 16–17, 20, 23, 24

Consultant: Raymond L. Puffer, Ph.D., historian, Air Force Flight Test
    Center, Edwards Air Force Base

1 2 3 4 5 6 07 06 05 04 03 02

Table of Contents

Chapter One

Learn About

➤ The AV-8B's mission
➤ AV-8B history
➤ AV-8B uses

The AV-8B in Action

Four Marine Corps jet fighters are lined up near an enemy country. They are waiting to take off from a 1,200-foot (366-meter) stretch of road. The fighters are AV-8B Harriers.

The first AV-8B starts to roll down the road. A normal jet fighter needs at least 6,000 feet (1,829 meters) of runway to take off. It would be traveling more than 150 miles (240 kilometers) per hour before it begins to fly. But the AV-8B travels until it reaches only 60 miles (97 kilometers) per hour. It then lifts straight up into the air. The other Harriers take off in the same way.

The AV-8Bs fly toward their targets at 600 miles (966 kilometers) per hour. The AV-8B pilots see a line of enemy tanks. Each pilot chooses a target and launches a guided missile. The missiles hit the tanks as the pilots turn back to their base.

Building the Harrier

In the late 1950s, the U.S. Marine Corps wanted jet fighters that could quickly provide air support. Marines often are the first U.S. military members to enter battles. The Marines wanted fighters to support ground troops as soon as they entered combat areas. But jet fighters needed long runways to take off and land. They needed to be located at an air base. The nearest air base often was located thousands of miles or kilometers away from the combat area.

In the early 1960s, Great Britain's Royal Air Force designed and tested fighters that needed little space to take off and land. These planes were called P.1127 Kestrels. The Marines first flew Kestrels in the early 1970s. Later Kestrel models were called AV-8A Harriers.

The AV-8B is designed to quickly provide air support.

In the late 1970s, airplane manufacturers built Harriers in the United States. Boeing, Rolls-Royce, and British Aerospace updated the AV-8As to make AV-8Bs. The U.S. military first flew AV-8B test models in 1978. The Marines began to use them for missions in 1985.

Today, the Marines have about 135 AV-8Bs in service. The Marines use two AV-8B models. These models are the AV-8B II and the AV-8B II Plus. Each plane costs about $23 million to build.

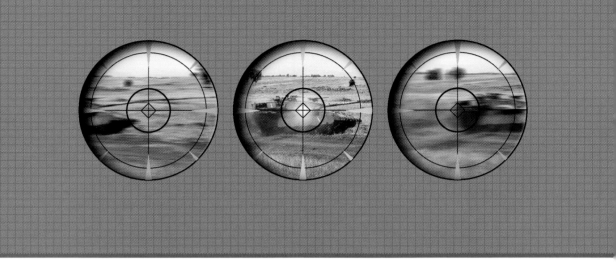

About the AV-8B

AV-8B Harriers are called jump jets because they need little space to take off and land. The U.S. military calls AV-8Bs vertical or short takeoff and landing (V/STOL) planes.

AV-8Bs can take off from and land in places other jet fighters cannot. These areas include short runways, grassy areas, and dirt roads. They also can take off from and land on small warships. Pilots usually try to land AV-8Bs on hard surfaces such as concrete pads. These surfaces prevent dirt, rocks, and other objects from entering the AV-8B's engine.

The Marines mainly use AV-8Bs for close air support. AV-8B pilots help protect Marines on the ground. But they also may shoot down enemy planes in the air.

The AV-8B can take off from warships.

Chapter Two

Learn About

- Engine nozzles
- AV-8B controls
- Body design

Inside the AV-8B

The AV-8B is shaped differently from other fighters. It has special features to help it fly vertically. Its wings are located on top of its body. They droop toward the ground. Other fighters have straight wings located at their sides.

   The AV-8B's large, oval-shaped air inlets are behind the cockpit. Air travels through these inlets and passes through the engine to help fuel burn.

Engine

A Rolls-Royce Pegasus jet engine powers the AV-8B. The engine uses oxygen to burn fuel. The burning fuel creates hot waste gases called exhaust. The exhaust rushes out of the engine's rear. The force of the moving gases pushes the plane forward.

The AV-8B's engine is large for the plane's size. It must produce enough power to vertically lift the plane as it takes off.

Most jet engines have one exhaust nozzle. But the Pegasus has four exhaust nozzles. Two nozzles are at the engine's midsection and two are located at the engine's rear.

Pilots can rotate the nozzles to allow the exhaust to flow in different directions. To take off, the pilots point the nozzles straight back to build speed. They then point the nozzles down to create lift. This force pushes the plane into the air.

To land vertically, AV-8B pilots point the nozzles down. This action stops the AV-8B's forward motion. The plane then hovers in midair. The pilots move the nozzles back as the plane lands.

Engine nozzles push exhaust downward to create lift.

This action prevents objects on the ground from entering the engine.

Pilots also can move the nozzles to change directions in the air. They may even move the nozzles to travel backward or sideways.

Jet Control System

The AV-8B has movable flaps on the wings and tail to steer it in flight. But these flaps do not work when the AV-8B hovers. The flaps need air to flow around them to work properly.

AV-8B pilots use a jet control system to steer the plane as it hovers. The engine pumps some of the exhaust into metal pipes. The pipes connect to the nose, tail, and wing tips. Small devices called valves are located at the end of the pipes. Pilots use cockpit controls to open and close the valves. The exhaust flowing through the valves causes the plane to change directions.

Body Design

The AV-8B's body is designed to help it quickly rise into the air. The wings are broader than the wings of most military planes. They also are rounded at the edges. These features increase lift.

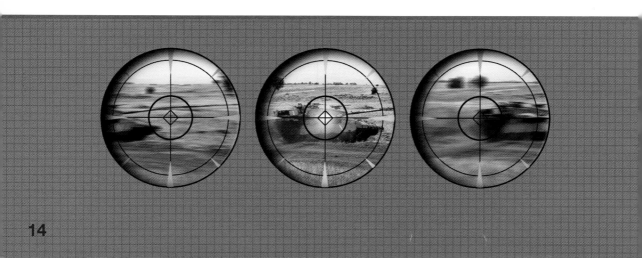

AV-8B Specifications

Function:	Ground force support
Manufacturer:	Boeing
Date Deployed:	1985
Length:	46 feet, 4 inches (14.1 meters)
Wingspan:	30 feet, 4 inches (9.2 meters)
Height:	11 feet, 7 inches (3.6 meters)
Weight:	12,500 pounds (5,625 kilograms)
Payload:	9,200 pounds (4,173 kilograms)
Engine:	One Rolls-Royce F402-RR-408 Pegasus
Speed:	629 miles (1,008 kilometers) per hour
Range:	1,600 miles (2,575 kilometers)

The AV-8B has a pointed nose to decrease air resistance. This force is created when air strikes a moving object. Air resistance slows down a plane as it flies. The AV-8B's wings also are angled toward its tail to decrease air resistance.

wing

fuel tank

tail

landing gear

fuel tank

The AV-8B Harrier

air inlet

nose

air inlet

wing

Maverick missile

missile launching rack

Chapter Three

Learn About

- Smart bombs
- Sidewinders
- Electronic equipment

Weapons and Tactics

The AV-8B can carry a wide range of weapons and electronic devices. Most of its weapons are designed to attack enemy targets on the ground. But the AV-8B also has weapons designed for air-to-air combat. Three pylons under each wing store bombs, missiles, or extra fuel.

Each AV-8B can carry external equipment that has a combined weight of more than 9,000 pounds (4,000 kilograms). The total weight of the equipment an AV-8B carries is called its payload.

The AV-8B may carry Maverick missiles.

Air-to-Ground Weapons

The AV-8B can carry a GAU-12 gun under its
body. The gun fits in a storage area called a pod.
The GAU-12 fires bullets from five barrels. Pilots
often use this gun to shoot at enemy trucks or
tanks on the ground.

AV-8Bs may carry other air-to-ground weapons. AV-8B pilots sometimes use Maverick missiles to hit small ground targets. Mavericks have a laser seeker. An AV-8B pilot or a Marine on the ground can aim a laser at a target. A spot of bright light called a laser beam then appears on the target. The laser seeker steers the Maverick toward the beam.

AV-8Bs also may carry laser-guided bombs (LGBs). These bombs sometimes are called "smart" bombs. LGBs may weigh up to 2,000 pounds (907 kilograms).

AV-8Bs often carry unguided weapons. They may carry cluster bombs. These bombs release small explosives called bomblets. AV-8B pilots sometimes fire CRV-7 rockets at ground targets. These rockets have an explosive device called a warhead in their nose.

Pilots usually dive close to the ground to drop unguided weapons. A screen in the cockpit called a head-up display (HUD) can help AV-8B pilots know where to drop these weapons. A bright line on the HUD shows the pilot where the weapon will land.

Air-to-Air Missiles

AV-8B pilots can fire missiles at targets in the air. One of these missiles is the AIM-9 Sidewinder. A Sidewinder has a heat-seeking device in its nose. The device guides the missile toward the heat from an enemy plane's exhaust.

AV-8B II Pluses can fire radar-guided AIM-120 AMRAAMs. Radar equipment uses radio waves to locate and guide objects. AMRAAM is short for "Advanced Medium-Range Air-to-Air Missile."

Other Devices

Other devices help AV-8B pilots during battles. AV-8B II Pluses have digital radar to help pilots locate distant targets.

A FLIR (Forward Looking Infrared) camera on the nose of the AV-8B II Plus detects heat in objects. It is connected to a screen in the cockpit. Pilots look at the screen to help them locate objects at night and during bad weather conditions.

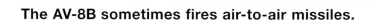
The AV-8B sometimes fires air-to-air missiles.

Chapter Four

Learn About

- Changes to the AV-8B
- Improved technology
- The Joint Strike Fighter

The Future

The Harrier has been in service for about 30 years. The Royal Navy of Great Britain first used an early version of the plane in 1982 during the Falklands War. Argentinean soldiers had invaded the Falkland Islands. This small island group is in the Atlantic Ocean. The Royal Navy used Harriers to help force Argentinean soldiers out of the islands.

Today, manufacturers no longer build new Harriers. But the Marine Corps still keeps them up to date. Harriers still are the only jump jets in service.

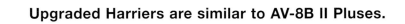

Upgraded Harriers are similar to AV-8B II Pluses.

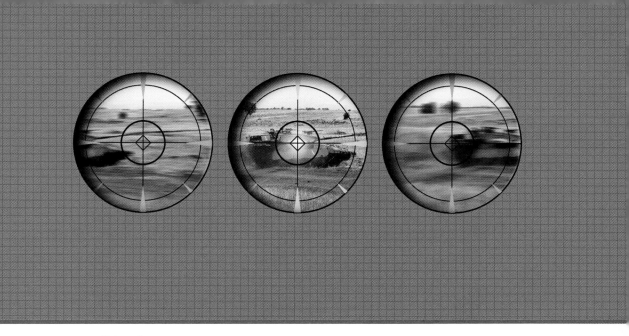

Updates

In the early 1990s, the Marines began a program to upgrade 72 of their older AV-8Bs. They placed more powerful engines, digital radar, and FLIR cameras on the older Harriers. They also equipped the Harriers with moving map displays in the cockpit. These screens help pilots keep track of their location. The updated AV-8Bs are similar to AV-8B II Pluses. The changes help the pilots fly at night and during bad weather conditions.

The Marines also are replacing some old AV-8B computers with commercial off-the-shelf (COTS) computers. These computers are easier to update and maintain.

The JSF will be able to take off as the AV-8B does.

Joint Strike Fighter

The Marines plan to replace the AV-8B with the Joint Strike Fighter (JSF). The U.S. Air Force and Navy also plan to use this plane.

In 2000, airplane manufacturers Lockheed-Martin and Boeing started testing the first JSF models. These planes will be able to take off and land vertically as AV-8Bs do. But they also will be stealth aircraft. These aircraft are hard for enemies to find using radar. JSFs also will travel faster than AV-8Bs.

By 2015, the Marines plan to buy about 600 JSFs to replace the last AV-8Bs. But AV-8Bs will remain an important part of the U.S. military until that time.

Words to Know

exhaust (eg-ZAWST)—the heated gases leaving a jet engine

laser beam (LAY-zur BEEM)—a narrow, intense beam of light

lift (LIFT)—an upward force created by an airplane

nozzle (NOZ-uhl)—a tube that directs the flow of an engine's exhaust; pilots can point an AV-8B's engine nozzles in different directions to steer the plane.

radar (RAY-dar)—equipment that uses radio waves to locate and guide objects

stealth aircraft (STELTH AIR-kraft)—an aircraft built with special materials and a shape that helps it avoid being detected by enemy radar

warhead (WOR-hed)—the explosive part of a missile or rocket

To Learn More

Beyer, Julie. *Jet Fighter: The Harrier AV-8B.* High-Tech Military Weapons. New York: Children's Press, 2000.

Green, Michael. *The United States Marine Corps.* Serving Your Country. Mankato, Minn.: Capstone High-Interest Books, 1998.

Sweetman, Bill. *Joint Strike Fighter: Boeing X-32 vs. Lockheed Martin X-35.* Enthusiast Color. Osceola, Wis.: MBI Publishing, 1999.

Useful Addresses

Marine Corps Division of Public Affairs
Headquarters Marine Corps
The Pentagon, Room SE-774
Washington, DC 20380-1775

National Air and Space Museum
Seventh and Independence Avenue SW
Washington, DC 20560

Internet Sites

AV-8B Harrier II Plus Joint Program Office
http://www.av8b.org

Boeing—Military Airplanes
http://www.boeing.com/defense-space/military

United States Marine Corps
http://www.usmc.mil

Index